# A LIFELONG SPIRITUAL WORK AS A FRIEND OF BILL W.

Ellie Lorenz

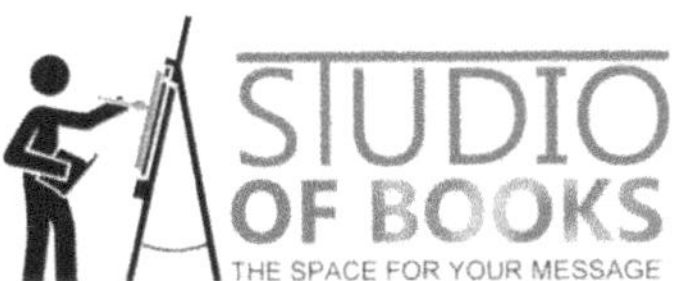

**Studio of Books LLC**
5900 Balcones Drive Suite 100
Austin, Texas 78731
*www.studioofbooks.org*
Hotline: (254) 800-1183

Ordering Information:
Special discounts are available on quantity purchases by corporations, associations, and others. For details, contact the publisher at the address above.

Printed in the United States of America.

ISBN-13: Softcover    978-1-970283-67-9
           eBook        978-1-970283-68-6

January 16, 2017, day one

The way it was, what happened, and what it's like now.

Today, the Lord put my unfinished book back on my mind. The first time he gave me this inspiration was in 1995-how many years ago was that?-and it is still unfinished. I completed the work back then, thinking, "Aww, good. It is done now. I can forget about it and go on with other things." I was wrong. I discovered the work that I had completed was a deep, soul-searching inventory of my life at the time. I was in my midforties, and as of yet, I had not nearly lived the most successful part of my life, so no, the work was not complete.

I woke this morning with the same agenda in my mind. If I am not quick to catch on to Jesus, my thoughts start rambling and drifting off into areas that are of no consequence and no importance at all in the spiritual world.

I have always been a day dreamer. When I was a teenager, I would spend hours and hours dreaming about meeting and marrying the love of my life. My world was one big fantasy about how that world would be. My day dreaming was an escape from a world I had no control over. I would crossover from a love scenario to a world of professionalism. I wanted to be a CEO of a big corporation and look out my high-rise window, which had a view of the city skyline. I really had no direction as to what I wanted to do with my life. Consequently, when I graduated from high school, I had visions of graduating from college and following my elaborate dream of becoming a successful professional of some nature. That did not come to pass. Instead, my life took a self-directed direction: early marriage and two lovely children.

Upon awakening this morning, I started mathematically reducing the bill I had been working on paying off. I like to do math in my head. It seems to be a diversion from the daily routine. When I'm not working on that, I watch the snow and think about how long it will be before the sun comes out and melts all the ice and snow, and where I am going to go to get out of the snow next year. I have been doing that ever since I moved here, which was 15 years ago, and I haven't gotten out of the snow yet. That's how my plans go.

Suddenly, I had this thought. If I didn't have the bills to calculate, and I didn't have the snow and the sun and the cold to concentrate on, what would I think about? The bills always go away, and summer will come. Everything that I think is important is of no value in life; it doesn't matter. It only matters if I am trying to control it, so why not keep a positive perspective and start the day with Jesus as my focus?

# TABLE OF CONTENTS

# CHAPTER 1

This year, I celebrate forty years of continuous recovery from alcohol. That, in itself, is a miracle and a mind blower. God has been faithful every step of the way.

He has been my guide on an incredible journey. In the early days of my recovery, I would hear, "If I had planned this, I would have never had an incredible life as the one I am having now." Proverbs 16:9 reads, "A man's heart plan his way, but the Lord directs his steps." Sometimes, He directs us without our help, although it makes it a lot easier and faster if we are willing to turn our life over to Him and give Him the reigns. Proverbs 20:24 states, "A man's steps are of the Lord; How then can a man understand his own way?"

The first steps I took to get into Alcoholics Anonymous were definitely God-directed. Believe me, it was a sure accident as far as I was concerned. I never laid in bed dreaming about AA or having a drinking problem or thinking, "Let me think, what do I want to be when I grow up? Oh, I know! I want to be an alcoholic." As a matter of fact, my first actual encounter with the program was a suggestion from a friend who was three years sober in AA. She suggested I call the central office of Alcoholics Anonymous to find out where the meetings were held. For the first time in a long time, I took someone else's advice and made the phone call as soon as I got off the phone with her. The person that answered my call was very kind and encouraging. He told me what meetings were close to me, and even gave me information about a women's meeting I could attend the next day. The encouraging part was when he told me to "finish my drink, and go to the meeting when that was done." I was encouraged, because no one had ever told me to finish my drink before.

This place sounded great, especially if they let you finish drinking. I was really thinking I was going to go to this place, and they were going to teach me how to drink socially without making a fool out of myself, and to stop blacking out and coming to in strange places. They were going to teach me how to handle this stuff.

Who was really in charge of my steps? For sure, God was, because of the incidents that led me to the door that Sunday afternoon, which was the day attended my first AA meeting. For about eight years, I had been living self will run riot, and the liability of it was not only catching up with me, it was running over me like a freight train. You know you're in trouble when you're sitting in the backyard of your aunt's beautiful home in Huntington Beach, California, sunbathing, listening to the ocean waves, and you shouldn't have a care in the world, yet it feels like all the problems of the world are on your shoulders. Well, that's where I had landed. The year is 1975, I am finally back in California, and I always believed I had to get back here to get my life straightened out. I had ideas of what that meant, but in all reality, I had no idea what the Lord had in mind for my life, or how He would play it out. The plans I had seemed to be leading me from one disaster to another.

As I sat there, I remember thinking if I walked into the ocean and started swimming, I would probably miss Catalina Island and not have the strength to get to Hawaii. I couldn't go forward and couldn't go back. There was nowhere to run and nowhere to go. I was twenty-eight years old, and my life was over. At that stage of my life, I knew the definition of hopelessness and desperation.

From the age of twenty-one, I had been making my living tending bar, so now that I was here, my next plan was to get a job "that would take care of everything." What I didn't realize was that I did have a drinking problem, and all this time I thought it was other people, places, and things. I had changed my places: I moved from Seattle to

Southern California; I left my troubles behind because 1 had come here to drink the way I wanted to drink and not have any of those people try to tell me what to do. Besides, what harm was I doing? Nothing that I could see. It was my life, I may as well have fun. Let's party! After all, hadn't I left all my cares and woes behind?

I don't know why they call destroying your life with drugs and alcohol a party. Some party, wouldn't you say?

Finding a job in my profession was a shoo-in. The reason I was a bartender was so I could have a good time and get paid to do it. Drinking was really an afterthought in the beginning. As a matter of fact, I didn't particularly like to drink. I had grown up with it and saw all the problems it had caused, so I never thought I would go down that road. I found a job, just as 1 planned, and I was once again living the dream. For a while, life was fun. Meeting lots of really neat people. Every day at work was like a party to me. I had eased up on my drinking, keeping it to days off, mostly. God was still guiding the steps; not necessarily to work in a bar, but in the relationships I had along the way, and the people He put in my path. I had just started work at the Safari Outpost when I met this gentleman whose son had just died. The day I met him, his grief and loss was so heavy. He had just came from burying his son. That day, we totally connected. We spent time talking, sharing similar losses; I had just buried my dad a few months earlier. Our friendship was instant. He became my best friend, spending lots of time palling around, laughing, drinking, and driving around in my giant four-wheel drive pickup. God always places protectors around me and I know "The King" was one of those people. He was probably in his sixties and I was in my late twenties. I can't explain our friendship, but it was so valuable to both of us. He was The King and I was Montana Mae. Burning the candle at both ends, partying hard, getting little sleep and working constantly, never stopping to take a breath, just run, run, run, the fun and games of the lifestyle I was living was taking its toll. My eight and a half years of drinking were catching up to me. Case in point: I experienced the first blackout that I was aware of. I had been out drinking, and I came out of the blackout on a dance floor in another town. That night was like all the rest of the nights. I was drinking after work, waiting for the band to start. The next thing I knew, I was dancing with a friend in a bar in a town that I had never been to. When I came out of the blackout, it was just like waking up, not that I felt like I was asleep. It's just hard to describe. We were dancing, everything appeared normal, except I was confused, concerned, and too embarrassed to ask where we were and how we got here. I had no idea what time it was, how long we had been there, where we were, or how we got there. It was baffling. I was good at acting as if, so that is what I did. The incident was very scary. I knew I had been in a blackout partly because I had seen my mother in a lot of blackouts, and she could never tell you what happened nor would she have any memory of the incident.

That was the first blackout that was real to me. There were others that just felt like hours lost, but not as scary as this. Another thing that was happening to me was that I was getting noticeably more and more careless, and doing reckless things. There is a passage for that from Proverbs 11:3, "The integrity of the upright will guide them, but the perversity of the unfaithful will destroy them."

I stated my drinking had eased up, and it did when I started the new job. I was careful to drink only when I knew I didn't have to be in control of my consumption. As the weeks and months went on, my drinking was increasing, I was using more and more, and I was getting more and more careless. I had a friend that was a patron who was genuinely concerned for my well-being. He told me I was drinking too much and asked me if I wanted to end up losing my looks and my youth sitting at the end of some bar, drinking my life away. Of course, I thought he was crazy and one of those people who should stay with his own party and mind his own business. After all, I knew what I was doing. I was having fun. With this in mind, I was unknowingly coming to the end of my career of bartending and living in the fast lane in sunny California.

## What happened?

My life went on like this until January of 1977. My pattern was to work all day, finish my shift and then start on the other side of the bar, as a patron. One night, I had drunk more than my share, the bar was closing, and it was time to go. I went to my truck and couldn't find my keys. I got in the back of the truck and dumped my purse upside until my keys fell out. I got back in the truck and took off. I headed for the restaurant where everyone gathered after closing time.

As I turned into the parking lot, I slammed into a steel pole. I backed off the pole, put the truck into four-wheel drive and drove into the pole again. My thoughts were, "Who did this pole think it was, getting in my way?" Not realizing that it was a stationary object, not just an obstacle that was stopping me. I had to have been in a blackout, or I had to have fallen asleep at the wheel. Either way, I was blessed I hit the pole and didn't drive into the restaurant. The collision did a great deal of damage to the driver's side. I couldn't open the door, so I got the passenger door open and came sliding out. A family was behind me in a Volkswagen, and they had observed the accident. The man from the car behind me wanted to make sure I was all right, so he came over to the truck and asked me if I needed help. I sarcastically told him I didn't need help, but my truck did. "Can't you see it's wrecked?" That poor guy and his family couldn't get out of there fast enough. He was probably sure he was dealing with a crazy woman. And sure enough, he was. Who else would drink like that and then get behind the wheel of a vehicle?

I went into the restaurant and called AAA and asked them to tow my truck. A friend of mine was in the restaurant and he offered to help, but I was drunk and belligerent and didn't want help from anyone. That was my drinking MO. This wasn't my first serious accident, but it was my last.

Somehow, I got back to my apartment. I don't remember how. I guess it wasn't important at the time. My Aunt Lauretta was visiting and staying with me for a couple of weeks. She was on the program I was on. Drink, drink, and drink. That night, she was with some people that had a scanner, and when they heard about the accident, she came looking for me. It was not funny, but a friend she was with had chains hanging from his pants or his arms. When they came in the door, the chains clanging sounded like hand cuffs, and I thought the police were coming in. I was sure I was going to be arrested, and the cops were going to take me to jail and throw the keys away.

Lauretta and I spent the next few days in the apartment; I was healing from the bruises, and thinking what a mess my life was at that very hour. We were talking. Actually, taking life seriously. In my mom's family, there were six sisters and three brothers. My mother was one of the older sisters. and Lauretta was the baby sister. She and I were eleven years apart. The year before my mom died, their sister, LaDean, a year older than Lauretta, had also died. She was only thirty-five years old when she died of liver failure due to alcohol dependency. The deaths of my mother and my Aunt LaDean were a big part of our conversation. This wreck was a wakeup call.

During that week, I told Lauretta I was not going to die in five years like LaDean. I was going to stop drinking, go back to Seattle, and spend time with my grandmother. Lauretta said she, too, would stop drinking, so we made a pact that we would clean up our act, get our lives straight, and meet back in Seattle at my grandmother's house in one year. Having set our goal, we decided to spend the rest of the week at places like Knott's Berry Farm, where it was alcohol-free and a safe place to hang out. There weren't many places that were alcohol-free, at least none that we knew about, since our lives were totally involved in the drinking culture.

Once the word got out about the wreck, some of my friends came, firemen and paramedics, to the rescue. Prior to the wreck, these were the guys that decided I needed a team to watch over me and try to keep me out of trouble. They were well aware of my drinking, so I became their project. For those who were off work, it would be their job to watch me and try to keep me out of trouble. It was a joke, but truer words were never spoken, I was in need of a keeper. They came and took the truck, put the Jaws of Life on it, and tried to straighten the body. They even tied the truck to a palm tree to straighten it out. After almost uprooting a few trees, they took other measures. They said that while they were trying to stretch this truck, a patrol car came by and watched, and couldn't believe what they were seeing, so they radioed ahead and had some more patrols come by to watch. They all got a good laugh and had a funny story to tell.

In a few days, I got my strength back and was ready to take off for Seattle. Lauretta and I reaffirmed our promise to ourselves that we would meet in Seattle in a year, and that we would both be sober. With that, I was off to Washington, and Lauretta was going back to San Diego. I made it to Sacramento, where my belongings were stored. I was going to collect them and get going on the rest of my journey.

Sacramento was God's new beginning for me. Little did I know that my life would do a complete turnaround, and that the events and years that followed would be a miracle. I arrived on January 13. The entire valley was covered in fog, it seemed. From the top of the Grapevine, all you could see was fog, and to me, it looked like smoke; like the valley had been on fire. Quite a change, leaving the ocean and eighty-degree weather for this fog covered place. I wasn't real fond of Sacramento, and this didn't help. It seemed like the fog never lifted. The first week in February was my first bender after Buena Park and the wreck. I remember, because I stayed in town and went through a few weeks of deep depression and desperation. I tried to stay sober, but I failed. Before I knew it, I was out drinking. I started on a Friday, with a bottle of brandy, Kahlua and a few pots of coffee. I remember how it scared me. Here I was, in a strange city, all alone, not knowing a soul, drunk-driving around in that condition, and I thought, am I insane? I tried to stay home, not go out, and not drive, but I found myself out again in the bar scene.

Saturday brought the familiar remorse. Hung-over, or sometimes not, depending on how much booze was in my system. In this case I was still drunk. I was having a pity party, because that is what alcohol does to me: it depresses me and makes me feel sorry for myself. Of course, after you have destroyed your life, you feel like you have the right to have a pity party. So, there I was, drinking and chinking. Always a bad idea. I decided to call the bar in Buena Park and head back to Southern California. It was Saturday, and all the gang would be at the bar, waiting for me to return to the party.

I called the bar, and Muriel, the bartender that relieved me on my days off, answered the phone. I asked her what was going on, who was at the bar, and if there was anyone knew. She told me she wasn't at the bar; she had found another job away from the bar scene, and quit working there a day or two after I left. I wondered how I got her number, since I didn't have her home number. Not only that, but she had moved since I left, so there would have been no way that I could have her number, yet there I was, talking to her at her home. This was not the first time God had switched the telephone wires on me. He did the same thing, the day I arrived back in California after leaving Seattle, a couple years before. He connected me to my aunt's home phone when I was at the bar in the airport, trying to reach friends who, at the time, were her neighbours. A man's heart plans his way, but the Lord directs his steps.

Reaching Muriel did not shock me or seem strange. I just accepted it, and went on with my conversation. We talked for a while, and she told me she was in the AA program and had been sober for three years. That explained why she never drank or stayed around after her shift. She further mentioned to me that, perhaps, I would consider going to an AA meeting. Her lead-in to talk about AA was to talk about the loneliness. She mentioned all the change she would give me to make those long-distance phone calls night after night, and asked if I wasn't tired of being sick and tired. I was most vulnerable at that moment, especially when she talked about my loneliness. God, in his infinite wisdom, knew when and how to carry the message to me. That was just what it took to get my defences down, and my ears to open and listen to someone about my drinking. I assured her that I wasn't an alcoholic, and she agreed. She merely suggested that I might like to attend a meeting and ease some of the pain that was in my gut. I was open to that, because I was sad and lonely and, who knows, AA might help with that, and maybe! could learn how to drink without getting drunk and be in blackouts all the time. As I looked back, it was as though she had to wait until there was a certain person who had to walk through the door, who she had to meet and carry this message to, before she could leave the bar and start a new life. Thank God, I was that person.

She told me that all I had to do was give central office a call, and someone there would talk to me about AA and share with me things that we had in common. This sounded like a good idea. I was hurting pretty bad. I was really feeling lonely and sad. I was sick of making all those calls after the bars closed in the wee hours, and having those ridiculous and embarrassing conversations, and then being reminded of them when you sobered up. Yes, she said a lot of things that I had been thinking about every time I drank and tried to get sober. I thought it was strange she knew so much about what I was feeling. Before she said goodbye, she said to look up the phone number for central office and ask them about a meeting.

As soon as I hung up, I called central office. An AA member answered the phone and began talking to me. After we talked, I was told what meetings there were. There was one that night, out in the area I was in, and there was a women's meeting the next day, Sunday, at three in the afternoon. I held that thought and wrote down the address. The AA person asked me what I was drinking and how much. I told them, and they kindly told me to finish my drink, and to go to a meeting when the drink was over. Wow, these people were awesome! No one had ever told me to do that before. Quite the opposite. Everyone was telling me to stop, not finish. I just knew I was going to like them.

Sunday morning came around. This is the one I mentioned earlier. It must have been a really bad drink, because I awoke so sick I could barely get out of bed to the coffee pot. It is like the song says, being so sick you can't hold your head up or down, or in any position that didn't hurt. I was thinking about that meeting, and all the reasons I couldn't make it. Luckily, it was in the late afternoon. It took a few hours, but I got ready and headed downtown. I found the address where the meeting was held. Across the street was a pancake house, so I went and had something to eat to try and get my courage up. Finally, it was time to go across the street. I had driven around the block several times. I finally parked, and forced myself to the door. The windows were all covered with curtains, so you couldn't see inside. After three or four attempts of walking away and then coming back, I finally pulled the door open and walked in. Fear was in my throat and all throughout me nervous system. This was a giant step into an area totally out of my comfort zone, especially with no booze to fortify my confidence. I quickly scanned the room to observe a few ladies sitting at the tables, drinking coffee and talking. Yep, just what I thought. What I was seeing were well dressed, well-coiffed ladies. They could have been at a luncheon at the country club. I thought, *Oh no, I'm at the wrong place again. This is not for me. These ladies don't Look like they've ever had a drink in their life, let alone ever had a history that goes with the alcoholic lifestyle.* Of course, Muriel never looked like she drank a day in her life either.

Once in the door, I spotted the coffee pot, so I tried to make my way, unnoticed, down the side of the room towards the coffee. I was hiding under a knee-length leather jacket, trying to be obscure, because I just knew every eye in the place would be watching me and judging me, which kept me in a fight-or-flight mode. I preferred flight, always ready to run. It isn't until later in sobriety that you find you're not the most important person in the world, nor are you the center of the universe. Wow, what a relief that was.

Coffee in hand, I found what looked like a safe place to sit: at the table, yet away from everyone. I was just settling in, when I heard a voice behind me, one with a southern drawl. "Hi, what's your name? I'm Betty Jean." as she hands me a cup of coffee and sits down next to me. The next thing she says is, "I know what kind of a drinker you are." I looked at her surprised and asked, "What?" She says, "You're a two-fisted drinker." and she laughed at her joke. We both laughed, which broke the ice from that moment on, and for some thirty odd years to come. What a day that was. It was one of the best days that I could remember.

That day was the first day of the rest of my life. I even became a member of the women's group that day. The things I heard and learned that afternoon were the first and greatest revelations I had for what seemed like the first time in my life. People talked about things that were never to be discussed by anyone in my family or anyone else's family. They talked about the things they had done while intoxicated, shameful things, things that made them feel guilty, things that were funny, sad, and disgraceful, and they were all able to laugh at themselves. When the women began sharing, I knew they had been everywhere I had ever been, and felt every feeling I had ever had. I was so excited to find people that understood. It had been so long since anyone had understood, that I had long since forgotten how to understand myself, and how to care for myself, and I had forgotten there were people that could care. They also expressed more wisdom than I think I had ever heard. I wondered if I had been raised under a rock somewhere. Why had I never heard any of these things, these many tools for living? It was really different from what I expected. I had thought I was going to go there, and they were going to teach me how to drink socially, and not make a fool of myself every time I wanted to "have a good time." Instead, they showed me that I wasn't the only person in the world who had been a drunk, and did the things I did that were incomprehensibly demoralizing. I no longer had to face this myself, alone and afraid, disgusted with where I had ended up in life. I found hope inside those covered doors.

The meeting was over by five. Betty Jean asked me if I was coming back. I told her I would if she would. I went home, walked in, opened the refrigerator, and pulled out a beer. Then I stopped, looked at it, asked anyone if they wanted it, poured it out and said, "I'm not drinking anymore." That was the end of the nightmare from hell, full of booze and willful destruction. But that was only the beginning of my road back. There was lots of healing to be done, lots of steps to take, lots of amends to make. There was growing up to do. There were emotions to face and change.

# CHAPTER 2

The first year of sobriety was the best year of my life that I could remember in a long time. I was thirty years old and excited about life for the first time since before puberty. I was having the time of my life. Everyone was so great, and they were so real, so open and honest. I was so exhilarated that I wanted to share my new found wealth with everyone I knew, so I would fly to Orange County every other weekend to take my friends at the Safari to an AA meeting. I got a couple of my friends to go to a meeting, but they became wise to me real quick and started hiding out when they saw me coming. I was shocked that they didn't want my newfound life. I couldn't believe that everyone in the world wouldn't want to live like this.

It was so great to not have any secrets, to have nothing to hide. In the past, my greatest fear was waiting for the other shoe to drop. It wasn't a matter of if, but when. I was learning that it was OK. That wasn't going to happen as long as I put sobriety first.

Betty Jean (BJ) was my new best friend in life. I clung to her like Velcro. That first cup of coffee she brought me sealed the deal. She had three years sobriety, along with the best sense of humor, and a positive spiritual program. She taught me so many things in the early years. She encouraged me to go forward and get involved in new things, like hospital and institution service work (H&I). The first meeting she took me to was a meeting held in the hospital, at the medical detox. She told me, later on in our relationship, that she didn't know what else to do with me, so she just took me with her to all her meetings. That night, when the people came into the meet-ing, they had on medical gowns, so to me, they looked like patients, which they were, but I hadn't figured that out yet. I was still way too foggy. I'd only been around a few days by that time. A few days later, we went to another meeting. This time, everyone had on street clothes. I asked her when the patients were coming in. She said, "We are the patients." It took a minute, but I got it.

At one of the meetings, she was sharing that she was trying to help me through some crisis, and someone said, "Why don't you give her to God?" BJ replied, "I do. I give her to God, but he works too slow and I have to take her back." One of the greatest gifts she gave me was taking me to the H&I meetings. I know it accelerated my growth in the program. You were to be sober six months before you could get involved; but because of BJ taking me to all the right places, introducing me to those already involved, and spending most of my time with them, I was able to get a clearance as soon as I had the six months of sobriety. I became one of the younger H&I mem-bers. That was really cool to be one of them. The older members, meaning the people with a lot more sobriety than six months, were very gracious to me and accepted me in all the H&I events.

When I was finally six months clean and sober, I was already a big part of H&I. The next step was to get me a background check so I could start going into prisons to take AA meetings to the inmates. The first facility was in Vacaville, California. Once a month, a carload of us would drive to Vacaville for the monthly meeting; the drive down and back was some of the best meetings for us. Lots of sobriety was shared in those trips back and forth from the prison. The second prison I was invited into was San Quentin in San Francisco. That was every five weeks for Sacramento to come in. I did that until I was almost three years sober. Not only were you taking the message, but there were lots of messages for us also. The reward and growth from sharing the message was immeasurable.

Year one of sobriety. That entire year was God's gift to me. A whole new life opened up, and I was on a pink cloud. Life was fun. It was an adventure. There was so much to do and so much to learn. I had so many friends, and living life sober was the greatest miracle of all. When I first got sober, I would ask myself what I was going to do with all the spare time if I wasn't drinking. You learn, soon enough, that there isn't enough time, and you wonder how you ever fit drinking into your life. I celebrated my first birthday in meetings all over Sacramento, and then to Garden Grove to celebrate with Muriel. I had a million questions to ask her about my blackouts, and bits and pieces of my life that I couldn't remember. She conveyed to me that it was not important. What was important was here and now, where I was and where I was going. She was a special angel. As life would have it, I never saw her again, but she'll always be in my heart.

There were a lot of ups and downs for the first year. They say that you go through everything sober that you went through drunk, and the good news is that you survive. I decided to move to uptown Sacramento. I didn't have a job, didn't have a car, but I did have some money hidden away. Maybe fifty dollars. I told BJ what I thought, and she said, "I don't think you can do that just yet. You need more time. No decisions for one year." I told her, "It's OK, BJ, it will be all right." She would say she was the one that was supposed to be telling me it was all right, but I'd be telling her. We had to laugh, because a guy in the program was an apartment manager, and he gave me an apartment deal which was five dollars off the rent. He thought it was a great deal. We knew better, but we were grateful at any price. It was great to have a place of my own.

# CHAPTER 3

Amazing things can happen to you in AA. It becomes a beauty parlor. I had this new friend in the program by the name of Carolyn. She and her brother were regulars at group three. They were both the sweetest people I could ever imagine; always happy, always smiling and always friendly. Recovering people are known for their resentments, but not chose two. They appeared grateful.

When I first met Carolyn, she was just getting clean and sober. She hadn't had time for transformation. Time went by. I wasn't paying much attention to anyone other than myself. After several months, Carolyn came into my view and I was astonished. "What have you been doing? What are you doing differently than me? You look so good and you sound so good." She says, "I keep telling you about my sponsor and what she is teaching me, and how I am going to a Women's Step study group, and how my life is changing."

I couldn't believe my eyes. They say, in AA, it's attraction rather than promotion. Well, I was attracted to what I saw, and I wanted what she had. I was not about to be left behind. Of course, she was so excited I wanted to meet Rhett, her sponsor, and change. She said, "I will tell her you are coming." Carolyn told me she had been telling Rhett about me for some time, and she was looking forward to meeting me.

I was finally convinced that I would go to a Women's Step study group to see what Carolyn was getting. Mind you, it wasn't the Step study that I was dragging my feet over; it was a Women's Step study. Before recovering, I found it hard to trust women. The people you met while running around frequenting bars were not the people who would readily reach out and love you unconditionally.

Carolyn became a very good friend and mentor. We were both working the same program, so we had a lot in common. Besides, she was married, had a husband, and was a homemaker as well as a business woman. Homemaker means "excellent cook, chef," and I had become a starving student who was always hungry and broke. It seems I was always around at dinner time. Carolyn was managing apartments. One day, I was hanging out at her place and she needed an apartment cleaned ASAP, so she offered me a job to clean it. That was the day I became an entrepreneur. The cleaning business turned into a landslide business. It was a sure way to get extra money.

While I was hanging out with her, we were out having lunch, and I decided I needed a job that paid cash. Cleaning apartments was good, but I wanted cash. I was never so broke in my life as I was after I got sober and started school. I had a brilliant idea. I was going to go bar shopping and find a job. That day, I walked into the second bar and I had a job that hour.

Can you imagine the delight Rhett, my new sponsor, had when she heard of my job? By this time, hardly anything I did surprised her, or anyone else for that matter. I can still see Carolyn tilting her head to the side, getting a slight smile on her mouth and a glint in her eye and shaking her head and chuckling, as if to say, "Oh my, oh my, here she goes again." Just wait until she sees Rhett.

The beauty of being clean and sober is the many people and new friends that come into your life. Carolyn and I remained friends for quite some time. We enjoyed years of growth and a new life.

Off I went to meet Rhett. I thought, "Well, I'll talk to her and decide if I want her to be my sponsor." I was used to running my own show, having my own way, and doing things the way I wanted them. Rhett met with me after the meeting. Little did I know, she was interviewing me. It wasn't me deciding if I wanted her to be my sponsor, she was deciding if she would take me on as her baby. When the meeting was over, she told me she would sponsor me. That's when I learned who was in charge, and it wasn't me. Imagine my surprise. Here I was, a little over a year sober, still thinking I had all the answers.

Rhett had a rule book. She had a list of do's and don'ts that you had to agree to if she was to sponsor you. Rule number two was no relationships for an entire year while you were working your steps. Now, any single, recovering alcoholic knows that is almost the most impossible rule there ever was. Who would come up with a rule like that and expect you to follow it? That would be Rhett, and brother, she was heart attack serious about it. Along with rule number two was suggestion number two: write daily and read the writings to your sponsor when you meet on a weekly basis. Have you ever tried to write honestly, yet leave out as much information as possible, especially changing a name here and there, or just leaving a name out whenever possible, wondering if any of this could make sense when you're reading it to your sponsor? It was quite a challenge. Try writing about resentments that you've just formed because you have a new or ongoing relationship that you're not supposed to have. Oh, the tangled web we weave.

About the ongoing relationship, she gave you time to work it out, but you better be serious about working your program. I had one of those relationships. His name was Bill D. I believe I learned more about relationships through our time together than any other relationship I had ever been in. Once, Rhett told me, when I tell someone no, they don't have to be told again. I often laughed at her point because I didn't know, at the time, that no was a complete sentence, no explanation necessary. Rhett formally walked me through the twelve steps of Alcoholics Anonymous. She taught me what they were, what they meant and how to apply them to my life. Step by step, I began to grow in spite of myself. Under her direction, I learned how to really trust another person with some of the most incomprehensible, demoralizing things in my past. Maybe they weren't to some people, but they were to me. She gave me the guidelines out of the big book, Alcoholics

Anonymous, on how to do a complete and thorough fourth step, taking a personal inventory of myself. It had five or six parts that you had to write out. Assets; liabilities; resentments; people, institutions, or principles with whom we were angry; a sex inventory; and fears. The entire list was hard, but the hardest one for me was the asset inventory. She had a list of assets that we were to write a little or a lot on, each one pertaining to ourselves. It was a real challenge to be able to say anything good about myself. I could write page after page on the liabilities I possessed, all the wrong I did, and all the guilt and shame I had, but it wasn't so easy to pat myself on the back or give myself an "Atta boy, good job." Not in the early days.

After the fourth step came the fifth step, which involved spending a couple of days with my sponsor, and reading to her everything I had written in this personal inventory. The thought of that, my friend, was scary. What will she think of me? Will she judge me? How can I tell all these secrets? It turned out to be one of the most freeing things I ever did. Rhett was a wonderful sponsor, and the best person I could have taken the fifth step with. She had spent so much time with me on a weekly basis that she knew me a lot better than I knew myself. She was there for me, always in my corner.

Step five. Admit to God, to ourselves, and to another human being the exact nature of our wrongs. Rhett and I went away for the weekend. She liked to have total private, quiet and secluded time to take the fifth step with her babies. For me, it was the scariest thing I could think of, having to go away and read my fifth step to my sponsor. To reveal all the things that I had written in that fifth step to another human being. It took a day and a half. The first part was the hardest. Assets and liabilities went by pretty fast, but resentments and the sex inventory, that took a lot of energy.

As we worked, she was there to discuss points with me as needed, but mostly she just listened. As we completed the next day, she showed me that I had created a list of people for my amends list for the eighth step, which is to make a list of all the persons we had harmed, and become willing to make amends to them all. Step six was right in there also: we're entirely ready to have God remove *all* these defects of character.

The sex inventory. This was a subject I didn't want to get into. As it turns out, the sex inventory is in there for a very good reason. It shows how sex, or relationship addiction, is such a large part of the addict's life style. I had learned there is a lot of cross addiction in an addict's life, and the crossover is very large in relationships. Of course, I didn't learn this on the day of my fifth step, but I was able to take the information and grow and learn from it. So many times, in all walks of life, problems in relationships can bring about pain that results in behaviours that are not always the norm for a lot of people. The inventory was a way for me to see my part in the relationship, and look at where I had been selfish, dishonest, or inconsiderate. Who had I hurt? Did I unjustifiably arouse jealousy, suspicion, or bitterness? All questions for a through, personal inventory. People in recovery have a lot of relapses over their relationships.

I thought the simplest inventory was the fears. I simply stated I was afraid of snakes, and that was all I could think of. I find that really funny today. I had no idea what fear was. I grew up being told not to be afraid of anything, so I hung onto that philosophy, thinking I was fine in that department. It makes me laugh, because Rhett never said a word about it when I was taking my fifth step with her. She just smiled and let me go on. As I became healthier in my mind and in my program, I came to learn that a huge part of the mind and life is controlled and touched by fear. There is a large section in the Big Book dedicated to fear because it is, and can be, such a stumbling block when it comes to one's recovery. Fear can stop you from discovering who you are in life. It can stop you from becoming who God created you to become. People limit themselves sometimes, because of trying to please other people, being afraid of "what people think of me." People that are fear-based are that way because they are driven by inferiority and insecurity. As you can tell, I had a lot to learn and a long way to go after a year's sobriety.

That day, as I drove away from the cabin, I was exhilarated, exhausted, and relieved. Most importantly, I was set free. I went to a meeting that night to share my wonderful experience. Upon returning home, I went to bed and slept as peacefully as a newborn. How wonderful it was to unload so many things that, in your mind, were the worst things in the world, and they made you believe you were the worst person in the world for having done them. It's funny too, because I heard this in a meeting, "You weren't that good at being that bad." I liked that.

I was about two or three months sober when I decided to get my real estate license. Having done that, and working as a realtor, it didnt take long for me to realize I could starve to death in this profession. I made my living as a bartender from age twenty-one onwards, until ! ended up in AA and got sober. I also worked as a teacher's aide for a while. Thar's when I decided I needed to go to college, get my degree and be the teacher, not the aide. I felt like I was doing the work, and the teacher was getting paid for my efforts.

One afternoon, Rhett and I were having lunch, and I told her I would like to join the Air Force. She thought that might be a good direction for me. You know all the rules and regulations that go with military life. That week, I went out to Mather Air Force Base to get a physical and begin my military career. I had to get up early for my appointment, so I didn't have a cup of coffee or a cigarette. The man taking my vitals couldn't get my blood pressure up. After three tries, he was turning white. - guess he was thinking he was going to have to send me to ER. I asked him, "What, no blood pressure?" I said that was normal for me. He suggested I have a couple shots of whiskey before I come back for the next physical. I assured him that they would not let me in any branch of the service if I had a couple shots of anything.

Another afternoon with Rhett, after one of our weekly sessions, she asked me what I wanted to do professionally. I told her I wanted to go to college. Her response was, "Well, let's do that. That's easy. Let's go to the campus and get you registered." Wow, I thought. Just like that. She made it sound like the easiest thing in the world, and to me, I thought it was a gigantic mountain.

I can still hear her excitement and enthusiasm when she would get a great idea. She would get a special note in her voice, a neat smile on her face and in her eyes, and you just knew she would make you make it happen, and she was always right there to help you any way she could.

College had been my dream since high school, and now I was really going to go. Rhett took me to the administration building to register for school. We spent a few hours getting all the information I needed and signing the necessary papers, and when the day ended, I was on my way to fulfilling my lifelong dream, and my grandmother's as well, of me being a college student.

Rhett took me by the hand and led the way. She was one of those miracles that God put in my life, a blessing in, oh, so many ways, not only to me, but to all those others she sponsored over the years.

Rhett continued to be a very important person in my life for a number of years. She became a very good friend. I was the one always on the geographical in life, but this time, Rhett moved out of state before I did. She left a legacy.

# CHAPTER 4

You don't turn thirty years of crazy thinking and insane actions into normalcy in two years, or in this case, five years. It takes time, clean and sober living and, for me, counselling. I discovered, once again, that God had a firm hand on my shoulder and was continuing to guide me when I would let him. Here I was, five years sober. I had a wonderful baby boy, who I thought would help fill the hole left by the separation of my older children, yet my life was not fulfilled. I was having a great deal of difficulty with depression. I just knew that I walked around with a cloud over my head.

It was like the song said, "Is this all there is?" I knew about the promises in the Big Book, and I didn't feel like I was getting them. I didn't feel joyous, happy, and free. I had worked the steps with a great sponsor, and tried to live life like I learned it was to be lived. Having done all those things, I still needed a road map. Even though I had God in my life and I had spirituality, I didn't have a relationship with Him. Furthermore, I still wasn't following the right guidelines, because I was still at the helm, running my own show.

Once more, I had a friend who was to guide me along the way: Mary Ellen. She had been attending a program called Adult Children of Alcoholics (ACOA). She was really excited about it and invited me to go, which I did, and again, life began to change. The biggest change was addressing, showing, and learning about frozen feelings. After being numb for all those years, not knowing those buried feelings were what was keeping me from joy.

After a few months of ACOA, she found a counseling group that specifically addressed these needs, and it was reasonable. The first interview I had with my soon-to-be counselor uncovered many issues that woke me up. She asked about my marriage and how long it had been before I knew it was in trouble. She asked about my first marriage, and how long before I knew that was in trouble. She told me about patterns, and how we had to learn to break them before we would be able to make healthy choices. I told her I had married two men, both with the same first name and the same last name initial. She called that a strong pattern model. I also talked about both marriages lasting almost four years, how both men were controlling, and how, each time, I turned my identity over to them. In the last one, I tried to keep peace and not make waves.

The other thing she told me was that there was a lot of grief and loss in my life. I had no idea. How can you have a life that is joyous, happy, and free when you have a lifetime of unresolved grief you didn't know you had? How do you get rid of what you didn't know you had? She told me she was surprised I had lasted five years without drinking. She said I was starting to do white knuckle sobriety. She was right. I didn't have a fear of drinking. I was afraid of blackouts. I'd already learned that I had done some pretty dangerous and stupid things while in a blackout, especially driving. That scared me to death.

Group counseling is where I continued to learn to trust, and to see and hear about blind spots in my life. We also wrote grief letters, or hate letters as I called them, which peeled off layers and layers of pain, sorrow; anger, grief and guilt. Lots of tears were spilled over those pages, and lots of new life breathed in.

Group counseling turned out to be the best therapy I could get. You had the benefit of all the other group members being there to give feedback. They could see and hear things that you alone would be blind to. They could point out areas that needed change, and areas that no longer worked in your life. You learned to trust your support system, which created a special kind of bonding among the group members.

From the time you get into AA, the first thing you learn about is resentments. What do you do with resentments? You learn you have to get rid of them. How do you do that? That is where forgiveness comes in, and for me and so many others, that is when you want to put the brakes on. "Oh no, I am never going to forgive so and so, after what they did to me, and what they put me through. No, no, never." Well, it doesn't take too long to find out that if you don't start forgiving, your life is never going to get better and it is never going to change.

Learning how to forgive is why AA had to be a spiritual program. You quickly learn you you can't do it yourself because of your humanness, so you have to find that higher power and ask Him to do it, to help you do it, and to make you willing to do it. My higher power was, and always has been, Jesus, even though I had many struggles with God-forgiveness, sin, guilt, shame, legalistic view – I always knew who my creator was. I just didn't know how to make the connection or, in my case, reconnect.

The time I was in group therapy was such a healing time. I wrote a lot of grief and loss letters, which opened my heart, mind and soul. By releasing so much hidden pain, sorrow, anger, rage, and all the emotions that get stuck and buried down there, you finally get to a place where you start to thaw out. All the buried emotions cause a person to become numb. Not only can you not feel the bad, but you also block the good. Good and bad feelings all become frozen emotions. The realities of frozen emotions have caused some people to turn to cutting just to try to feel something.

Early in my AA years, a few of us got together and had a good old AA party. That meant a ton of coffee, and lots and lots of conversation. I was sharing part of my story when my resentment towards my mother came out of my mouth. I stated that I hated her. I was raised that to say anything bad about mom or dad was taboo, so my statement was worse than terrible. Once it was out, there was no taking it back. I was so embarrassed and horrified that I spoke such a thing. I was also giving away family secrets, and that was really unacceptable. Once I started group therapy, I discovered there was a beautiful thing that came out of that statement. I learned how profound it was towards healing my relationship with her, and finding that part of me that was also part of her. She had died when I was twenty-four, so there was grief and loss over her death that was unresolved, but there were years and years of childhood grief that goes along with being raised in a home where alcoholism is part of the environment. My letters freed me from the resentments. They allowed me to see my mom as a person, as a young woman with skeletons of her own. I came to understand her, even have lots of empathy for her and all the pain she had to deal with during her young life. I became fee to love her and realized that I never hated her; I hated the alcohol and what it did to her as a person.

# CHAPTER 5

An unhealthy relationship and/or a dysfunctional marriage can bring resentments and anger that you would have never known could have happened. A disgruntled spouse or significant other might steal from you, take serious legal action against you, and try to do bodily damage to you. Domestic violence can happen with the one that was supposed to love and care for you.

It's been over fifty years, and this is still the hardest, most painful part of my story for me, for my eldest children, for my loved ones that lived through the heartbreak with us, and later, even my youngest child, who lived with me while I continued to carry the grief over the children I never got to raise and be with. I include it because of the grace, love, favor, guidance, and protection that God has given me throughout my life. If I had been without the Lord, I would not have survived any of this.

Going back to the time when our life became completely shattered, and our family destroyed, I always believed my kids and I would get back together. I knew we would get past all this insanity and be a family again. In my early years in AA, people would tell me that I would have my kids again, that we'd be a family again. My family told me the same thing.

It's amazing, the things you find out or figure out later in life. The biggest shame I had was having to tell anyone that I had lost my children in the divorce. I always felt I had to give an explanation as to what happened because I was ashamed. To tell the truth, I didn't understand how the cards turned against us the way they did. I thought I had it all figured out.

I was seventeen when I got pregnant with my daughter. Thing at home were falling apart and I starting making my own plans base on fear and from thinking, "What is going to happen to me?" I real, made decisions based on self, of course. What else do you do when you see the walls falling down around you and you can't see a safe haven? | never wanted to get married, but I figured if you had to, you had to. This was way back in the day, when things were done properly if you were in "the family way." Well, that was the beginning of my rocky road. We were married when I turned eighteen. We had our first battle at the reception. I left him once, when I was still pregnant, then again, when my daughter was two months old. We had another physical battle. This time, it became very brutal. This time I became afraid for my life.

Four years passed. I had a son, my husband had a good job, and we were living the dream. There was only one problem with that: I was in a very dysfunctional relationship. I knew better than to talk to "strangers." My husband's jealousy was intense, and it only grew with time. Anyone who has been down this road knows the life, and the dialogue that goes with it, and so it was with us.

I had been in this relationship since I was twelve years old. There was a short break in my senior year, but that didn't last. At last, there was a chance. I was to go to my Aunt June's college graduation in Long Beach, California. While I was in California, I felt like I had been released from prison. It was the first time I had been away from my then-husband since I was twelve years old. I was finally free and, like a bird out of a cage, 1 began to soar. I was with my aunts and my cousins, and the party was on.

One of my favourite things to do was to go to Oceanside and dance at the Normandy with the marines.

Aside from running to the Normandy, we ended up having endless pool parties at the apartment in Long Beach. I was a twenty-year-old living the teenage years I had missed. Also, I was a non-drinker, so it was pretty innocent on my part. My aunt, my grandmother, and my cousins were always with me, so I didn't see that I was doing anything wrong. After all, it wasn't as though I was dating any of these people. I had enough sense to know I was married —just not enough sense to remember who I was married to, and that he had a totally different perspective than myself. I realize now that people who are that young can be very impulsive and not think things through to the end.

I had an amazing couple of weeks. I didn't want to go back, and I knew I had to find a way to get away from where I was. I had no idea that I was behind a wall of black depression. Once I got back to Washington, I took a part time job down from my house. It was nice to be able to work. I had never worked for anyone before except my parents. I liked earning a paycheck.

Prior to this, me and my girlfriend, I will call her BJ One, were discussing writing to the troops and cheering them up. Her husband was retired military, and he had mentioned it. I told her I would have to meet someone to write to them. Well, guess what? The opportunity was right around the corner. My Aunt Lauretta lived not far from Oceanside, so every chance we got, the girls would drive to Oceanside and dance with the marines.

We take a lot of what we learn from home into the world with us. My dad and mom were very gregarious people. Their home was open to all comers. I grew up that way. That's where I got into trouble, not knowing the difference in people. BJ One and I were out shopping one Thursday, the only day the spouse was off work, which was a little detail I forgot about. Besides, I never thought about the mail nor was I concerned about it, but that day, every letter in the world came in from Vietnam. Those dancing marines had our addresses, and they wrote. When we got home, there was the spouse, sitting on the steps of our house with a handful of letters in his hand. You know how you know what you know? I asked BJ One to take the kids to her house, got out of the car, got to the front door, and that was the beginning of the end for all of us. There was a terrible fight.

I got beat up pretty bad. I finally got into the bathroom and locked the door. He must have come to his senses because he didn't break the door down. This goes to show how immature and naive I was. I really wanted to read the letters and get all the news, because after all, these were my friends, and we had shared some good times. I was just like a teenager because, in a lot of ways, I was still a teenager—twenty isn't that old. Your brain doesn't fully develop until age twenty-six. I did read the letters, and it seemed there was a lot more going on in sunny California than I knew about.

That evening, I went to work. My boss saw me when I walked in. He wanted to know what happened, but I was too ashamed to tell him. He wanted to take pictures, and again, I wouldn't let him. I was so naive and uneducated. I didn't have a clue what would happen to me, my kids, and the rest of their childhood and teenage years. The husband drove me in my car, to and from work that night. When we got back to the house, I sat down at the dining room table. He sat across from me and tried to make conversation and started laughing. I guess he had just dismissed the tragedy and figured all was well and wonderful. Who knows?

I went to bed. The next morning, I woke up and every tangible thing in our lives was gone. My car, all the vehicles, the check book, the savings book, any means that would allow the kids and me to make a clean get away. I called my Aunt LaDean, who came and got the three of us and my dog. We went to live with my grandmother.

Over time, we talked about divorce. I wanted my kids on weekends, holidays and summer vacations. After two years of arguing, threats, stalking, and more threats to get the kids and keep them away from me, he verbally agreed to let me have the kids on the above terms.

He already had the house. Because I took the kids and fled, he later used abandonment as a custody issue. I wanted the house because the school was practically in the kids' backyard. They would walk a few feet and be in school.

After the kids were with him for that first school year and we had made this verbal agreement, as soon as the school year ended, he and his girlfriend packed up the kids and moved to Bellingham. So much for the gentleman's agreement. That was what my dad raised me on. He said that a man's word is his bond. Little did I know that everybody didn't know that. Years later, I processed so many of the earlier events to try to make some sense out of everything that happened. After I left, I never gave a change of address. It never occurred to me, so when the notice of the divorce hearing was sent out, it must have gone to my old address. At any rate, I was never notified, and I was divorced a year or so before I knew anything about it. By my not being at the hearing, I never had a chance to fight for my kids. I was so ignorant about everything. I had no idea the world worked like it does.

In the beginning, I made two appointments with two lawyers. One told me to go home, keep my mouth shut and do what I was told, and life would be good. This was in the summer. The second attorney told me to kidnap my kids when they came to stay with me for the summer. She told me just to keep them, and not return them to their father when it was time for them to go back to school. Like a fool, I took her advice. We had a great summer. We knew they were going to stay with me. We were looking forward to our life so, after the summer break, I didn't give them back. I almost ended up in jail for kidnapping my own kids.

I had just found a decent attorney that had just started working on my case that week. On Friday, he called to tell me there was a warrant out for my arrest. I had to surrender my babies. I had to turn my kids over to their father and stepmother that day at three in the afternoon. I didn't believe that something like that could happen. Kidnap your own babies? I'll always remember that day as clear as if it was yesterday. It was a cold, blustery, rainy day in Seattle. We were heartbroken and devastated. Not only was it my birthday in October, but the kids and I had just buried my father the month before, and now we had to leave each other again. Three years after my mom died, I was, once again, numb and going through the motions. I even had to sneak the kids into the funeral home and into the funeral, because I was trying to keep them. It took me three months to recover from that episode. The kids were crying, I was crying and we were clinging to each other for dear life. It felt like life had just imploded on us.

They were begging me not to let them go. What can you do? I was so powerless. There was nothing I could do for them.

It was raining that day. Really miserable, gloomy, and depressing. We walked into the building, and there, the perfect little family was sitting, waiting for my children to be handed over. I think, by that time, he had two little girls with his new wife. What did he need with my babies? How can I describe that day? There are no words to describe the unbearable pain of having to let your babies go, especially somewhere they didn't want to be. I had to turn them over, say goodbye, and walk out that door without them. I felt like I would die. I was no good to them. I couldn't help them. I could only think of the trauma they must be going through, having no control over their lives, and I had to hand them over to the enemy. That was the beginning of the endless, sleepless nights, crying and worrying about the welfare of my kids. The drinking really escalated after that.

I guess the next step was typical of a person who has been beaten and defeated. I let the deceiver tell me my kids would be better off without me, and that I should stop interrupting their lives by bringing them home with me every summer. I felt I was always keeping them in turmoil. My dad's death seemed to end my time in Seattle, with my kids at one end of the state. With my parents gone, I decided to take off and go back to California, and try to find my life. I had told myself I would be doing my kids a favor if I got out of their lives and gave them a chance to make stable lives for themselves. What a stupid idea that was. That had to be one of those ideas Satan plants in your brain to destroy you and your kids. I really believed that I was disrupting their life by taking them away from their friends every summer and moving them around with me when we were together. I wanted to stop the grief. When we were together, we were so happy, then about three weeks before they had to go back, all the sadness would return. All the pain, the grief, and the tears. I believed I could stop that if I went away. Please, don't anyone ever do that. Those kids will always need you. Leaving them was the worst thing I could have ever done.

# CHAPTER 6

The day came for me to leave. I told my grandmother I would be a short geographical, I ended up in Sacramento. I was really lost by this time.

My life was a blur. All I wanted to do was disappear, drink until I couldn't drink anymore, and then stop drinking until I couldn't stay stopped any more. I finally decided to make a run down south. I wanted to get to the ocean. I had friends in Huntington Beach who would open the door for me if I wanted to come back. I headed for the airport and was on my way.

Years started to pass rapidly once I was back in California, and my children were in Washington State. When we did get together, they were growing up and getting their own identities, their own friends, lives that I wasn't a part of. As far as I was concerned, they were still my babies. Time hadn't moved on for me. I was still holding onto the idea that we would walk out of the nightmare and have a life together, the way it was meant to be. They were my flesh and blood. All that kept me going through all the struggles. They were my hope. I was two and a half years sober, and my children were now teenagers. I had worked the steps, and had completed two years of college. My life was going good, except for that aching in my heart I didn't know how to fill. I had not learned about ACOA or family recovery; all that was still ahead of me. There was so much I didn't know, and the key words here are two and a half years sober. I was still so far from making sound decisions and choices. I was running on emotion. They had grown up quite beautifully, and I was really proud of them, but we were not united as a family.

# CHAPTER 7

I had just returned from what was to be my last summer with my grandmother in Seattle. It was Thanksgiving 1979, and I was at an Alkathon, in group three, when I first met who was to be my second chance at having a family. An Alkathon is when the group has meetings and food for twenty-four or thirty hours during the holiday season. It's a place for those who don't have a family to share the holidays with, especially those in carly recovery, and those who are most vulnerable. For me, it was my family, and I was there to take part and support.

I met Larry quite by accident. It was a whirlwind relationship. I don't think it even was a relationship. I don't know what to call it. At any rate, we married, not because I was anxious to tie my life up again. I had been single for twelve years, and for all those years I was not looking for a commitment, but somewhere, I had this harebrained idea that if I had a baby, I could fill the hole in my gut, the empty feeling in my heart, and maybe, just maybe, I could get something back. The funny thing is that I was really happy doing what I was doing; being involved in H&I work, going to prisons and carrying the message of AA, going to school fulltime, working on my degree, and having good friends. Life was good, but I didn't have my family. I had this notion that if I did get married, I would turn my life around and make a home for me and my kids. Boy, did I get a wrong number. That never happened. Instead of getting easier, life seemed to get more complicated.

My son was born on his due date, June 30. He was a strong, strapping, beautiful baby boy. I called him God's miracle to me. His first ten days of life were horrific. He had a fever the doctor couldn't find. They ran every test on him, including a spinal tap. What a terrible thing to have to happen to a new born. Every day, I would get to the hospital and sit with him as long as they would let me. I had just had surgery, and couldn't drive, so my wonderful mother-in-law would drive me to go see our boy. She was a godsend. I love that lady to this day. She was Justin's grandmother and, in so many ways, my mother. She would say, "I don't see how he can be sick, he is the biggest baby in the ICU nursery." He weighed nine pounds and ten ounces. He looked like a baby giant in the incubator next to all the preemies.

After ten long days and nights, I got to bring my boy home. It turned out he was born with an ear infection, brought on by too much fuid in his ear. After all that grief for all of us, it was finally over. It was a day of celebration, one that lasted for twenty-one years. Justin was the joy of my life. I got to share in his growing up. I got to see one of my babies grow up, and I got to experience his transition from childhood to adulthood. I got to be with him through all of his experiences: his years of being Superman, of being crazy about He-Man, of moving on to baseball from T-ball, to making the team in high school—he was Mr. First Base. In high school, I asked him to stop playing. I was concerned about his high blood pressure. He was always agreeable to what I would ask. Maybe he was so busy trying to please me that he never had a chance to know what his own life should be. From baseball, he moved to drama, when he was picked up by the drama coach. He was a winner, and the drama couch was always thanking me for him being in her class, and not in baseball. I was at every rehearsal, every play, just like in baseball. For all those years, it was like a fairy tale life. God gave me a son that gave me unconditional love. It was a glorious season. Justin graduated college, married, and went on his way. The season was over. He grew into a fine young man, and a wonderful, proud father. He gave me two grandsons. Before he found his way back, Justin and I were estranged for a few years. Again, God was there to carry me through the rough times that were ahead. And one Mother's Day, there was a miracle phone call from my son. God answers prayers.

# CHAPTER 8

Life's journey takes many twists and turns. We never know what is waiting around the next comer. The beautiful thing I have found in Amy life is that, with God's strength and the faith he has given me. I have been able to go around those corners and continue to grow, change and try to be all that He created me to be. I can't say it hasn't been a story out of Danielle Steele's books from time to time, because it seems like it has. There was a time when I wondered who was writing my life story. I don't think I would have planned so many of these extraordinary events. I do know that all the time I spent in recovery made me strong, brought me more faith, and gave me the courage and the fortitude to withstand all the trials and tribulations that life has brought and continues to bring, only on a smaller scale.

When I share my story in AA meetings, I would tell my friends that I would want new recovering mothers to know they might not ger their kids back. It doesn't always happen. It didn't happen to me, and that was important to know, because your sobriety cannot depend on circumstances, but on your relationship with God, the one who formed you in your mother's womb, the one who loved you from creation, who breathed life into you, who saw you and said: this is good. I found that whatever life throws at me, I can catch and go with, because my journey is about traveling the road I was created for. It's not for me, not for my family or my friends, not for my education or my job, not for fun or profit. It is for my Creator.

The miraculous part of my life is that God always kept people around me that were there for me, people that would protect me, guide me, and help direct me when I would take direction. In all that I experienced, I always had a lot of loving, caring people at my side. There were many years before AA when I was anything but lovable. I had so much anger.

Alcohol became my bitter enemy, not my beloved friend. I was no poison out of a bottle. I had a friend in AA who told me, when I first came to AA, that he thought I had just gotten out of Folsom prison because I looked so angry. I felt like I could have been an inmate. As recovery began to happen, I would wonder how and when I got like this. I wasn't like this as a child, but I do remember becoming a very angry teenager. Most importantly, I wondered if I would ever overcome the anger, if I would change or if I would always be full of hate and discontent.

Little did I know, but God sent me another one of those special people. This was in the early 1970s, when I met Joe. Within a short period, we began dating. He never told me what to do, never criticized me. He was satisfied with whatever crazy scheme I came up with. He wasn't jealous of my friends. If I wanted to dance and be crazy, he would go along with it. On top of all those qualities, he was a really nice person. How refreshing it was, meeting someone as special as all that, who liked me just the way I was, who had no interest in changing me, as had always been my experience. He just accepted me. After a few short months, he was gone, back to California, and I was left to do whatever it was I did. As time went on, I left my job in Seattle and moved on to new expeditions. We lost touch.

Twelve years later, and guess who comes back into my life? I was in family counselling for about a year and a half. Larry (Justin's father) and I had ended our marriage that year. One of the important details was to close relationships so one could move on in life, and I knew Joe was an unclosed relationship. Now the opportunity had arrived for me to do just that. I had always known where he was. I was just afraid to call him and talk to him. Rejection, fear, and abandonment ran deep in my veins. I called him, and to my surprise, it was as though he was waiting, or at least expecting the phone call. How that conversation went is another chapter. I asked to meet with him, thinking this is what I needed to do for the closure of a twelve-year-old relationship. It turns out we both had been clean and sober for the past eight years. We stopped drinking at the same month and year, eight years earlier. When you haven't seen someone in twelve years, it would seem strange to be sitting at that table across from him, but it was as though we were sitting at the same table we last had dinner at in Seattle, twelve years earlier.

Justin was four years old when Joe and I got back together. Joe, Justin, and I went for our honeymoon in Hawaii. We were a family. I was right, for a change. Joe has been the rock in my life. He taught me how to trust in a relationship and what it is to be secure. I set down roots, probably for the first time since I was that little girl in Montana. Life became stable and secure. The rollercoaster had stopped. I became a stay-at-home mom to raise Justin and help Joe run our business. Life was finally becoming normal.

# CHAPTER 9

Well now, no so fast. What is normal? With my living environment stabilized, I thought, "I can finally breathe." At thirty-seven, I began having excruciating pain in my shoulder. It was so severe that it caused nausea. I couldn't sit, lay down or rest, and it always started around ten in the evening, and lasted until the next day. Usually, when the gur-wrenching pain ended, I would begin to fear for when the next one would happen, and if I could be able to stand it.

After three years of doctors and no diagnosis, I asked my son's paediatrician to look at my hand. He immediately suggested that I go see his friend, who was a rheumatologist. I had rheumatoid arthritis. For the next decade, I spent a lot of time being sick and adjusting to the chemotherapy drug that works to stabilize the disease. The good news is that I went into remission around the year 2000. I took myself off the meds, although it returned in 2005 but not as severely: It was manageable. Those years were scary. However, they did wonders for my spirituality. Pain can be a real catalyst to moving one in a spiritual direction. I knew I had one chance at recovery, and that would be Jesus. I also believe those years were very stressful for my son. He was always afraid I was going to die. It could have caused him to make choices he might not have made. Only he and God know the answer to that. God is faithful. When the time came, he gave me two more wonderful people in my life. Suzanne and Lloyd became my neighbours. They arrived in Sacramento from Calgary, Alberta, which made them like family to me. I was raised next door to Alberta. I practically grew up there. I had a lot of family there, namely my great-grandmother and my grandfather. Suzanne and I had a spiritual bond, a lot like the first BJ in my life. We also shared the same crazy, wild, magical curiosity, both loving adventure and exploring new horizons. We seemed to make it our goal to go and explore every chance we got.

One of those quests led us to a Christian fellowship that would literally change both our lives. Suzanne had lots of friends. One of them was a wonderful lady who led her to a church, which eventually led her to another church where she began to go to bible study. She would share with me what she was learning, and it sounded so awesome that I wanted to learn everything. Carol is a truly anointed bible study teacher whose gift of teaching transformed us. Believe me, we both needed transformation, much to our surprise. Only after a few years of being under the guidance of Carol were we able to see where we had been and where we are now. The major word I heard was the word of healing. I believed I would go and find out for myself. I did get healing in so many ways. I believe it was that faith that allowed me to go into remission with the arthritis. It surely prevented me from becoming terribly deformed and crippled from the disease. I have been grateful for the spiritual blessings I've gotten from this disease, because it really led me to a deep trusting relationship with Jesus. There are so many ways to heal, and for me, spiritual and emotional healing was my victor.

# CHAPTER 10

Miracles come when you least expect anything to happen. A lot of times, for me. I received miracles and didn't know it was a miracle.

God never gave up on getting my attention, He can be very creative at times, and sometimes he just clobbers me with whatever is handy, which at times feels like a Mack truck.

The year my mother died was most eventful and chaotic. The bar where I began my first career as a bartender, and where I found my new family, suddenly collapsed on March 23, 1972. It was around nine in the evening. I was talking to my cousin, Marino, when the phone went dead. The lights flickered and went out, and there was dust coming in. The bar was packed. A friend of mine was celebrating with a few others because he had just sold his classic car which, by chance, was parked outside when the crash came. Guess whose car was demolished?

It was a blessing that everyone got out of the building without incident. That was one of those miracles that go unaccounted for. Thanks to the bar caving in, I was now unemployed, which was also a blessing because I was ready for a little vacation.

I spent more time with my parents, my kids came home for the summer, and I was with them. That summer, I was helping my parents. We were at the laundromat, washing and warming the stools at the bar next door. I had one too many Brandy Alexanders and got wasted.

As I was driving down the freeway, enjoying the sunny Seattle day, I got pulled over for speeding. Things accelerated, and before I knew it, I was on my way to jail, or so I thought. I knew they could only hold me for four hours and I'd be out. Not so. They took me back to the station in Georgetown and kept me until ten in the evening, then they took me downtown and booked me. What an experience. One I hope never to have to repeat.

August came, and my aunt and uncle came to visit. They were on vacation, so they took me with them. I went back to California with them, and enrolled in college. I knew I had to get on with my life; college was the plan.

I had to appear in court for the DUI on September 7, so back to Washington I went. Of course, as soon as I got to town, the party was on. I had my apartment, but I didn't know the phone was disconnected. On September 12, my Aunt Naida came to the door to tell me that my mom was in the hospital. I went there, but she didn't wake up, so after a while I went home to shower and change before going back to be with her. I lay down for a minute before I dressed when, all of a sudden, it was like an electric shock went through my body. I jumped up and said, "Oh my God, my mom." Just then, my landlady came to the door and said my uncle was on the phone. I asked him, "When did she die?" He said she died just minutes ago. She died that evening, having never regained consciousness, the cause of death being alcohol induced.

Her death brought on a downhill slide. I crawled into the bottle and did not want to get out. I was in so much grief, and had no way or knowledge as to what to do with it. I had been carrying so much that it all just piled up and came down on me like an avalanche.

I was living at my dad's house. I gave up the apartment because I thought I was headed back to California. My poor dad, he didn't know what he was in for. I was no good to him, myself, or anyone else. By this time, my kids were back with their dad, so he had just me to contend with.

I was sleeping in my mom's room when I was awakened by someone in bed with me. As I began to wake up, I realized it was my mom. I was sleeping on my side, and she was up against my back with her arm around me while holding my hand. I knew the feel of her hand so I knew it was hers, plus she was wearing a diamond pearl ring that we shared.

She said she had to tell me something. I asked her what she was doing here, because she was dead. She said she needed to talk to me. What she told me was that I had to stop this drinking and take control of my life. I told her that I didn't get a chance to tell her goodbye and I wanted to kiss her goodbye. She said, "Don't turn over." which I did anyway, and in that instant, she was gone.

When I fully woke up, it was like the room was in a blue-white haze of odorless smoke. I jumped out of bed and ran to my dad's room. I cried like a baby for a long time.

When I went to court, I lost my license for six months because I refused a breathalyser when I was arrested. I thought I knew more than they did. Well, they showed me. Hurting, and with my life really out of control, a friend came along and found a job for me, so off to work I went. He was kind enough to taxi me back and forth to work. I stayed off the sauce and resumed my good work ethic.

From there, I was offered a job in North Seattle. I got my car back, and away I went. Here, I met a man who was reading *The Late and Great Planet Earth* by Hal Lindsey. That book changed my spiritual life. I was reminded that I was saved by grace. I had placed that truth on the back burner. It was that truth that gave me hope. This happened several months after I had that vision of my mom.

I was so excited about the first book that I read the second one. *Satan is Alive and Well on Planet Earth*. In my early twenties, I was so unhappy with the way my life had turned out that I was looking for every avenue I could find to escape. I found my way into astrology, a very dark avenue of the occult.

The wealth of information in this book was captivating. I was hanging on to every word. One night, I came home from work, got my book out and set the mood to read. I put on a black nightgown, lit a green candle, and placed it on the coffee table in front of me. On the cable to my left was a lamp that sat on a cast-iron base with three legs. On the walls on each side of the couch were knickknack shelves full of knickknacks. The scene is set.

I was learning about the occult, fortune telling, horoscopes, Ouija boards, and all sorts of black magic things that go against God. I was engrossed in what I was reading, when suddenly, several things began to happen at the same time. The lamp next to me began to spin on its axis so fast you couldn't stop it with your bare hands. Candle wax spilled all over the front of my night gown. Knickknacks flew off the shelves, hit the door and landed on the floor. The place looked like a whirlwind or a hurricane had passed through.

I wasn't able to figure out how long the incident took. It seemed as though I had just sat down and started reading when this happened. I got up, went to the phone, and called my grandmother to tell her what had happened and to start praying for me. While I was talking to her, I looked out the window, and it looked like it was daybreak.

I wasn't afraid. Intuitively, I knew what was happening, who was behind it and why. Later, I was telling my Aunt Naida what happened, and asked her if she wanted to read the book. She said, "Are you kidding? No way." I knew; for sure, I was seeing and hearing for the first time in years. I guess I would say I was beginning to awaken.

In '75, I decided that if I could get back to California, I could find out where my life went sideways. I thought my kids were doing all right where they were living, and I also thought I kept disrupting any chance they might have to have a stable, secure life if I kept dragging them around. Both my parents had passed on and, except for my grandmother, I was pretty much through with Washington State. When I was going into the fifth grade, my parents separated.

They had a ranch and a business in Montana and, due to a series of circumstances, they parted, and I went to Long Beach, California to live with my Aunt June and Uncle Mike. It was the best time in my life that I can remember, sort of like being on a working vacation. There was lots of love. I was in a great Catholic school. In the morning, we would line up to pray outside, and you could smell the sweetness of the ocean air. There was sunshine. We also lived across the alley from the beach.

That time was short lived. My parents got back together and brought me back to Washington. In the meantime, all our earthly belongings were stolen from the ranch in Montana. Everything. Even the animals that my dad thought were being taken care of were either dead or gone. So, this is where I got the mindset that I had to get back to California. It took me from 1955 to 1976. Life is a journey. I left for California in the spring of 76, I stored any excess baggage I had in Sacramento, boarded a plane, and headed to Long Beach. Once again, life had gotten pretty chaotic for me, and the drinking hadn't helped. My only focus was to get on that plane and order a drink. Much to my dismay, none other than a Catholic nun, dressed in a full habit, sat down next to me. Well, here I was, a little Catholic girl. It was like sitting next to the Father, and Mother Mary.

I wasn't about to have a drink in front of her.

No problem, I thought. We were changing planes in San Francisco. Once she got off, I'd be free to drink. So, I get off the plane, walk into the restroom, and whose voice do I hear behind me, asking if I was going to Long Beach, and if I could show her where to go to catch the plane? I almost died. Off we went to Long Beach.

That was some trip. On the way down, she started to tell me my life story. She was telling me how bad it had been, and how things were going to turn around, and that life would be all right. I thought to myself that it was going to be all right, that I was going to the marine ball, that I would meet some high-ranking officer, get married, and live happily ever after. Into my fantasy, I escaped.

What was mystical was this. She had given me resources to reach her if I ever got back to Sacramento: the church she was with, her phone number etc. She was meeting her sister at the airport and, in those days, Long Beach was a small airport. You landed on the tarmac and walked inside to meet your people.

She got off a couple of people before me, so I hurried to catch her, but she was nowhere to be found. Neither outside nor inside. She was in a habit, so she couldn't be missed. She was wearing a nun's cap that looked like the one on the old sitcom The Flying Nun. I thought that it was weird, but I dismissed it, and went to the bar to finally have that drink.

Originally, I was going to Huntington Beach to see old friends that lived next door to my Aunt June. They had given me an open invitation that, if I wanted to, I could stay with them. After a couple of drinks, I went to the phone to call them. The phone rings, and my aunt answers the phone. I did not want to see her, or anyone else from my family! She recognized my voice and wanted to know where I was, while I wanted to know what she was doing at the neighbours' house and answering their phone. She said, "I'm at home." I said, "You can't be. I don't have your number." Again, she wanted to know where I was, so I reluctantly told her I was at the airport in Long Beach. She said, "I will be right there to get you."

Later, all I could say was, "Thank You Jesus." That phone switch, as I call it, more than likely saved my life. My aunt was my role model all my life, and God knew just who to send to get me out of my own way.

When I moved back to Sacramento, I tried to look for the nun and the church, but there was no such person or place.

I consider my wrecking my truck a miracle. If that hadn't happened, I would have gone on living the insane journey I was on. It made me realize that I was really flirting with death, or worse, legal problems. Once that took place, I decided to go back to Seattle and take care of my grandmother, or she would take care of me. Once again, God was directing my steps. I had to stop by Sacramento to pick up what I had stored there. Sure enough, once I fell off the two-week wagon, I was off and running again.

The miracle in that was calling the Safari in Buena Park and getting Muriel on the phone. Another switched phone call. I asked her who was at the bar, and she said she didn't work there any longer. She got a job on the day I quit and left town. I wasn't surprised, even though I never had her number.

Had all those instances not taken place, I never would have met Muriel, who was also a bartender at the Safari Outpost. The best part was she was a friend of Bill W., and directed me to the program.

The first meeting I attended was a miracle, as was meeting BJ, and deciding that very day that I was a non-drinker. The desire to drink, along with any craving, was lifted from me from that hour on. I never again had a need to drink.

All the people God put in my path, who led me towards the best sobriety and spirituality one can have, were all used by Him to get me to where I am today.

After I had been sober a while, and was learning to follow the Lord, good things began to happen. There were more and more awakenings in the spirit. Every morning, I would go outside, lay in the sun and listen to the Christian radio station. I was learning about the Bible. This one morning, I was getting settled in my chair and just starting to lay back when I verbally spoke out, saying, "I guess I am going to go to my grave with this ache in my heart for my kids." As I said that, I laid down, and i was as though two hands reached down and lifted off my chest what fer like a barbell used in the gym. I knew it meant I no longer had to be burdened and worried about my children. The pain was lifted off my chest. They were in high school. One was to graduate, and the other was right behind her. They were now young adults.

Another spiritual experience happened when JK was almost two years old. I went with a few friends to an AA Christian charismatic conference in Oakland. I walked into the church, into a mass that was being held on the altar. We were all gathered around the priest, praying. I opened my eyes and all the people on the altar were dressed in robes like those in Jesus's time. I closed my eyes and reopened them to see if things were normal. They were not. They were still in robes and praying. The next thing I saw was this hand stretched out to me. I thought how great it was that Jesus was showing me that he had the same color as me, a beautiful golden bronze.

Then the mass ended. We all left the service and started into the foyer when my friend and I got to the priest. He put his arms around both of us to greet us when we both started to weep. We wept for so long that he finally pulled us out of the line and sat down on a couch with us. We continued to weep. It was like the Holy Spirit's rain, cleansing and healing. Finally, we stopped crying, said good night, and went to our rooms. That was the first time since JK was born that I wasn't afraid I was going to lose him. God assured me he was mine and he would be all right.

This was a three-day conference, and the three days were filled with one miracle after another. The next morning, I went to a rebirthing session. The meditation takes you back to being inside the womb. As I was being led outside the womb, I was there with Jesus, who was gently coaching me to come through the birth canal. I didn't want to come out. I didn't want to be born. I know God has a sense of humor because He got me to the door, opened it, and I pushed Him out and closed the door. H laughed and said, "No, that's not how we do this." This time, He carried me through the door. Once outside the womb, I was holding the baby; which was me, and He told me to hand the baby to the person who had hurt me most in my life. There, standing around were my mother, father, my biological father, and others. The person I handed the baby to was my biological father, who I had never met in my life. I was very reluctant to hand the baby over, but Jesus had His hand on the baby, and he told me it was all right because he would always have His hand on me, and the baby. That was the oddest outcome, but it turned out to be so true. My biological father had hurt me most in my life because he abandoned both me and my mother when she was carrying me. The wounds she carried kept her from being the loving, intimate mother I always wished I had. The grief made her life very sad, and it eventually led to an early death with the help of alcohol.

On the third day, we had a morning meditation. We were walking on a beach, and there was a gentle warm breeze blowing on us. I was walking down the beach with Jesus. He had His arm around my shoulder, and we were just enjoying the pleasant, refreshing morning. It was a glorious day.

Later that day, on our way home, my friends and I were sharing the events of the past three days, and I shared what I experienced on the beach. I shared that it was as though Jesus was with me, and He had on a long robe with a braided gold rope for a belt, and my friend chimed in and agreed, and His sandals were tan, and the gold braided rope hung down to the bottom of His robe. We both stopped talking and looked at each other in awe, because we had the same experience and we weren't anywhere near each other. What an awesome God I serve.

The next huge miracle in my life was meeting my friend Suzanne. We were both searching for our spiritual roots, and we found them together when we met our bible study teacher, Carol. She taught us the Word of God. She was our mentor and our greatest friend. We were so blessed to sit under her teaching, and she had the greatest patience with us, because we were like two wild burros that knew nothing. As it says in the Bible, she took us from drinking milk to eating meat. That is to say, we grew into adults spiritually.

I had two physical healings. The first was when I was new in AA. The signs and symptoms were there. I was having problems talking for short periods of time. I would have to stop talking, cough, and catch my breath. It was as though my throat was very tired. It turns out I had a goiter somewhere in my neck or throat. I went to the doctor, who examined me and sent me to get another exam, which included drinking colored fluid. When my results got back to my primary doctor, there was no sign of a goiter. He was baffled. He said, "You definitely had a goiter when I sent you to get the x-ray. What happened?" I told him that the only thing I did differently was that I had a lady ask to pray over me, and the goiter was gone. He never questioned me.

The next miracle was in '98. I had gained a lot of weight from taking the medication to overcome my rheumatoid arthritis. When my stomach started to bloat, I thought it was just part of the weight gain. Suzanne and I were on a mission. We had both taken in foreign exchange students, and we were on a sight-seeing trip to San Francisco. I kept complaining about my stomach, so we both figured it was gas, or something immaterial. We were walking up and down the hills trying to relieve the gas, when she suggested rice tea, so we went to Chinatown to get the rice tea, which didn't help. The next day was the fourth of July. The kids were all going out to see the fireworks. My husband was fixing a door in the family room while I was sitting at the table working on paperwork, and my stomach was continuing to bother me. It was about six in the evening when I told Joe I was going to go to the ER and see if they could do something to get rid of this gas. "Don't worry, I'll be right back. If they're busy, I won't stay."

They took me right into the exam room, and before I knew it, there were doctors and nurses hovering over me. The next thing I knew, they were sending me down for an MRI, then putting in an IV, then another MRI, then a catheter, and in all that time they had told me nothing.

I told the nurse, "I know enough to know an IV, a catheter and two MRI's are more than nothing." My husband was getting really worried. I called him a couple of times, with updates of what I knew. He wanted to come down, but I told him he couldn't do anything but wait, and he needed to be there for the kids to get home from the fireworks.

Around two in the morning, they told me that they were admitting me to the hospital. I called Joe, who was frantic and could only expect the worst. I told him I was admitted and if he could call my aunt. He said, "I'll call her right now." "No," I replied, "it's two a.m., all she can do is worry or pray. Call her at seven a.m." My aunt was on the first plane out, on her way to Sacramento. Surgery was scheduled for Monday morning. It turns out my gas and distended stomach was from a tumor that was growing as we spoke.

Again, I had a room full of doctors preparing me for anything that could happen. I was to have a nine-hour surgery. From what they could see, the tumor was attached to all the organs, which was about as bad as it could get.

I called Suzanne. She wanted to know where I was since I wasn't at the fireworks. I told her I was in the hospital and asked her if she could please call our prayer team and get the prayers for healing and recovery going. By that afternoon, my room was filled with prayer warriors praying around the clock. Suzanne and another friend, Marie, sat in the waiting room and prayed all during surgery. JK had been at a church holiday that weekend, so we didn't tell him until he got home that night. He and my aunt stayed with me on Sunday night. JK led me around the halls, following me with the IV. He was so worried. I told him that God hadn't brought me this far just to let me die and not complete my mission. I knew I was going to be fine; besides, things were happening so fast that I didn't have time to be worried or scared.

My aunt is a nurse and an administrator in a hospital in Ventura, so she told the doctors that I would be in worse shape than I was already in if I had to be on a cold gurney for hours during surgery, so she saw to it that they put me on a heated one. Who knew? I had no idea you could do that.

The surgery went on for two hours, not nine. The tumor wasn't attached to anything, and there was no cancer. They had to take it out in one piece for fear of it being cancer, and that cancer spreading. That's how they knew it was twelve pounds.

When I went back for a post-exam, the doctor told me that he was sure glad I made a liar out of him. They knew for sure that it was malignant. I said, "The power of prayer. Thank you, Jesus."

Our move to Washington State was a miracle. I would never have come if it wasn't God's purpose for us. My husband and I came to Washington for a family reunion. He liked it so much that he wanted to retire here. I went along with the idea, thinking it wouldn't be a problem. It took us ten years to get relocated, and once we arrived, the reality set in as to what we had done. We pulled up our roots in California, and came to the Northwest. Even though I had gone to school in this part of the country, I seemed to have forgotten about the snow, and just how cold it gets here in the winter.

We had been dragging our feet getting out of Sacramento, when I finally hear God's voice saying we had to go, and we had to go now. I believed Him. I came home, told my husband we had to get this house on the market, and go. The house went on the market, and within three days, I came home and saw a "Sold" sign over the "For Sale" sign. I just about died. This was real.

Once we were here, I realized I needed to go back to school to get a profession. A degree is nothing without a profession. I found myself traveling a hundred and twenty miles back and forth to school when I was only four miles from the university in Sacramento. But the reality is that I would have never left Sacramento if I had started my career there when I first graduated from college, and God needed me to return to Washington State, because I had a lot of unresolved issues that I had swept under the carpet when I hastily left the state in 1976.

God has worked me through all those issues, along with letting me reconcile with my children, and getting to know my grandchildren and great-grandchildren. He also has given Joe a longer life than he would have had in California. We know God saved his life by moving him here and getting him into a clean climate.

Yes, there have been many miracles in my life. People, places and things have all been miracles in one way or another. God has used all these things for my good. I have been blessed, not because of myself, or anything special about me, but because of God and how much he loves me, and how much He loves all of us. What He has done for me, He wants to do for each and every one of us. That is His undying love, His long suffering, and His tender mercies.

# ABOUT THE AUTHOR

At the age of thirty, Ellie W. (Lorenz) found her way into Alcoholics Anonymous. The spiritual journey is about learning how to walk with the creator in a spirit of obedience, which was totally foreign to her.

Miss Ellie had lived in rebellion and with an I-will-do-it-my way attitude for most of her teen years. She received a lot of her role modelling from her peers on the Blackfeet Indian Reservation, where she was raised until the age of nine and a half.

Jesus had always been in her life, but she put Him on the back burner once she reached puberty.

AA was her catalyst to a way of living that transformed bet entire life. The Lord used people, places, and things to guide and direct her steps, all of which were directly placed to get her to where she is today.